YOUR KNOWLEDGE HAS VALUE

- We will publish your bachelor's and master's thesis, essays and papers

- Your own eBook and book - sold worldwide in all relevant shops

- Earn money with each sale

Upload your text at www.GRIN.com
and publish for free

Bibliographic information published by the German National Library:

The German National Library lists this publication in the National Bibliography; detailed bibliographic data are available on the Internet at http://dnb.dnb.de .

This book is copyright material and must not be copied, reproduced, transferred, distributed, leased, licensed or publicly performed or used in any way except as specifically permitted in writing by the publishers, as allowed under the terms and conditions under which it was purchased or as strictly permitted by applicable copyright law. Any unauthorized distribution or use of this text may be a direct infringement of the author s and publisher s rights and those responsible may be liable in law accordingly.

Imprint:

Copyright © 2017 GRIN Verlag, Open Publishing GmbH
Print and binding: Books on Demand GmbH, Norderstedt Germany
ISBN: 9783668384897

This book at GRIN:

http://www.grin.com/en/e-book/351854/the-study-of-sensitivity-in-relationships-in-jhump-lahiri-s-unaccustomed

Sumitha Stevenson

The study of sensitivity in relationships in Jhump Lahiri's "Unaccustomed Earth"

GRIN Publishing

GRIN - Your knowledge has value

Since its foundation in 1998, GRIN has specialized in publishing academic texts by students, college teachers and other academics as e-book and printed book. The website www.grin.com is an ideal platform for presenting term papers, final papers, scientific essays, dissertations and specialist books.

Visit us on the internet:

http://www.grin.com/

http://www.facebook.com/grincom

http://www.twitter.com/grin_com

'THE STUDY OF SENSITIVITY IN RELATIONSHIPS' IN JHUMP LAHIRI'S UNACCUSTOMED EARTH

SUMITHA STEVENSON

ABSTRACT:

The world reels in the various upheavals that have lashed the world at large. Modernization churned with growing relationships, everyday and hour has destroyed the loyalty and submission in relationships at large. Gone are the days when sincerity and devotion in relationships were prime and sublime. We seldom know who to blame for this tremendous downfall- the people or the scenario in which they are placed , blown up egos or the changing times or trends.

This paper is an attempt to clasp the importance the novel by Lahiri who happens to be one of the English language's most celebrated commanders, a storyteller revered for her perfect discreet realism and crisp directness of words . It is a humble attempt to study the sensitivity in relationships of the migrants with emphasis on Jumpha Lahiri's – Unaccustomed Earth. Being a child of Indian immigrants Lahiri stresses on the Diaspora events, people and relations. The word Diaspora has been taken from the Greek word which means 'to disperse'

> 'Diaspora', is the voluntary or forcible movements of peoples from their homelands into new regions …..[Ashcroft,Griffitd,Tiffin]

Diaspora is the communities of people living together who

> "acknowledge that the old country as a nation often buried deep in language,religion,custome or folklore, always has some claim on their loyalty and emotions". (qtd.in.kaur,192)

The "Unaccustomed Earth", is a series of short stories revolving around the Diasporas' - their worries, struggles, relationships and good as well as sad events of their lives. There has been a wave of series of relationships in these stories which lack sensitivity and thus leading to turmoil and urge to keep or break up with the existing ties.

KEY WORDS: Diaspora, relationships, sensitivity, culture.

Contents

ABSTRACT: 1

I. INTRODUCTION: 3

II. CONCLUSION: 12

References: 13

I. INTRODUCTION:

Jhumpa Lahiri who was born to Indian emigrants from West Bengal, brought forth the best acclaims in the field of literature. She was the one who first meticulously experimented with stories about Indian immigrants trying to adjust to new lives in the United States. In between all her short-form gems came the less graceful debut novel, "The Namesake" (2003), which had its biggest moment when transformed into a Mira Nair movie. The Interpreter of Maladies, (1999) which won the 2000 Pulitzer Prize for Fiction, seek love beyond the barriers of culture and generations. Then the eight stories which appeared in Unaccustomed Earth (2008) take us from Cambridge and Seattle to India and Thailand, as they explore the secrets at the heart of family life. The Lowland was shortlisted for the National Book Award in 2013, the Man Booker Prize 2013 and the Bailey's Women's Prize for Fiction 2014. All these publications have manifested the tone of Diaspora in accompaniment to layers of relationships and the lives of people whom she talks about in her stories. She moved to the United States at the age of two, after she was born in London, and aptly comments

> "I wasn't born here, but I might as well have been." [Minzesheimer, Bob. "For Pulitzer winner Lahiri, a novel approach", USA Today, 2003-08-19]

She talks about the conflicts of being a foreigner in a new country which she had to call her home. Her focus remains on the identity crisis and sense of belongingness. She refers to disliking her name in the novice part of her schooling –

> "I always felt so embarrassed by my name.... You feel like you're causing someone pain just by being who you are.[Anastas, Benjamin. "Books: Inspiring Adaptation", Men's Vogue, March 2007]

Jumpa portrays many aspects of India and people who immigrated to countries abroad, even though she did not stay in India, yet she dares to unfold many true aspects of the emigrants. At times she has been referred to as a "distant author," who indulges in details which could be untrue. Yet her stories have made a remarkable impact and have received a world wide acclaim. Writers find great inspiration in the lives of the migrants. Being a migrant, as stated by Salman Rushdie is "a ball hurled high into the air, with massive potential and possibilities".(*"The satanic-verses"* .www.enotes.com). Amitav Gosh also deals with the element of Diasporas in his famous work- 'A sea of Poppies', a novel set during the pre-opium war period. The famous ibis trilogy – Deeti, who was supposed to burn herself in the funeral pyre of her husband. But Kalua, manages to help her escape that fate and both escape to Mauritius only to face more trials. Diasporic literature may be mindful of the ancestral native land, but the nostalgia for it has lessened, if not disappeared. And diasporic literature is, moreover, engaged by the possibilities of the new location.

Lahiri brings her experience of the Diaspora in her stories, with references to families who have migrated from India, most of them from Calcutta. The urge to keep the Indian roots alive, still dominates the lives and homes, of the first generation in a foreign country. The constant urge to root the children to their traditions and culture is also reflected. In spite of all these constant reflections of Lahiri's life the stories and conflicts are in no way a self experience. As stated by Lahiri in her interview, -

> "I don't know if other writers face this, but I come up against it again and again, people constantly assuming that everything is for real and everything happened to me. I mean, if everything I wrote about happened to me, I would be a very strange creature."[CWW].

There have been many acclaimed writers who have dealt with the theme of Diasporas. As very aptly stated 'Migrants with their diasporas identity occupy a curious position that is a great site of great opportunity.'

Lahiri portrays various characters with sensitive relationships in "Unaccustomed Earth". The series of stories have characters who delve into bound relations, or happen to fall into a relationship due to attractions, love or naturally. Only few characters live up to their relationships with dedication, while majority of them tend to fall in and out of these bindings.

All kinds of relationships in the novel - Parent and child relationships, marital relationships Vs Secret love relationships, pure love relationships , secret love relationships, sibling relationships- go through numerous upheavals during the course of the story. Some succeed while some fail, whereas some succeed and yet fail in the hands of fate.

The Parent Child relationship is strangely depicted in the chapter "Unaccustomed Earth". Ruma who is pregnant with her second child is awaiting the arrival of her father at her home in Seattle. Her only correspondence with her father in the past thirty eight years, were the post cards which he sent while on his visits to different places. The messages on it reflect no words of love and fatherly feelings. It was Ruma who took the responsibility of calling up her father, after her mother's death. The conversations were brief and limited to general talks. Now that her father was coming to visit her, Ruma felt an air of discomfort. She could not resign to the fact of taking care of her father, with whom she did not have close ties unlike her mother. She feared

> "that her father would become a responsibility, an added demand, continuously present in a way she was no longer used to." (7 UE)

Ruma is reminded of the days she cried, when she learnt that smoking could kill, and that her father too smoked. She asserts that,

> "He had done nothing, back then, to comfort her; he'd maintained his addiction in spite of his daughter's fear." (21 UE)

There is a constant battle within Ruma to receive and reject the fatherly feelings of her father. Her fathers' advice to Ruma, to begin working after she has her baby, is not taken too well by Ruma. She reflected that she could have convinced her mother on this issue easily, rather than her father. There are times Ruma is surprised by her father's gestures; times when he took care of Akash, bathing him, playing with him and preparing a nursery in the garden for him too. These were little things which she had not expected of her father.

A similar bond of father and son is bought about in the chapter, "Year's End", wherein Kaushik misses the presence of his mother, who is no longer alive. His father breaks the news of his second marriage to Chitra, a school teacher; she was nearly twenty years younger to his father. She had been widowed with two girls, Piu and Rupa. The news makes Kaushik want to revolt, but he accepted the decision with resignation and tried his best to be kind to his father. To quote,

> "I said this more as a challenge than out of politeness, not entirely believing him." (254 YE)

As the story progresses Kaushik tries to be in his best of behaviour to the new members of the family, trying to bond with them. But, eventually the memories of his mother keep haunting him, in the house which once belonged to his mother. He says

> "I was suddenly sickened by her, by the sight of her standing in our kitchen. I had no memories of my mother cooking there, but the space still retained her presence more than any other part of the house." (263 YE)

Kaushik's love for his dead mother and his hatred or dislike towards Chitra and her daughters burst out, when he finds the two girls busy with the open box of his mother's photographs, which had been sealed and hidden after her death. This infuriates Kaushik to an extent that he spits out venom at the two girls, who were petrified. To quote -

> " You have no right to be looking at those, they don't belong to you." ------"Well, you have seen it for yourselves, how beautiful my mother was. How much prettier and more sophisticated than yours. Your mother is nothing in comparison. Just a servant to wash my father's clothes and cook his meals. That's the only reason she's here, the only reason both of you are here." (286,287 YE)

These lines are a pure indication of the hatred Kaushik had for his father who had got a new wife after the death of his first wife. The anger towards his father is directed towards Chitra and her daughters indirectly. The inherent hurt and loss weakens the ties of Kaushik with his father.

The Secret Love Relationship seems to be evident in " Hell – Heaven". It is a one sided love affair between the narrator's mother referred to as 'Boudi' and Pranab Chakraborty a "brilliant student, who had come to America to study engineering at MIT." Pranab Kaku as the narrator addressed him was a regular visitor, who would come starved at all times and would eat regularly at their home. 'Boudi' developed a secret liking towards Pranab which seemed to be one sided. As the narrator, the daughter remarks,

> " I did not know, back then, that Pranab Kaku's visits were what my mother looked forward to all day, that she changed into a new sari and combed her hair in anticipation of his arrival, and that she planned, days in advance, the snacks she would serve him with such nonchalance. That she lived for the moment she heard him call out "Boudi"! from the porch ……..."

The drag relationship of the parents seems to be the reason that the wife seems to nurture a secret love for Pranab. The Marital discord is evident in the husband and wife relation. They had married only because the father wanted to placate his own parents. He only loved his work, his research and preferred solitude. Further on 'Boudi's' secret love crashes into jealousy for Deborah, whom Pranab had fallen for and wanted to marry her too. There are constant moments which reflect sheer jealousy for Deborah. At the engagement she commented to her friennds, -

> "She will leave him,".... "He is throwing his life away." (73 H-H)

Gradually 'Boudi had accepted the fact of her love being betrayed and she continued to live her solitary life at home, avoiding any meetings or outings with Pranab and Deborah.

Another episode of a Secret Love relationship develops between the protagonist Hema and Kaushik, in the chapter – "Going Ashore". Hema is to marry Navin very soon. But, she seemed to have invented a lie, to stay in Italy and spend time by herself in the month of November. To basically take advantage of a colleague's, "empty apartment in the Ghetto." It would be in January when she would get back to Calcutta to get married to Navin. There seems to be a void in this alliance. As the story progresses, Hema happens to meet Kaushik through a common friend. Kaushik was a photo journalist, who travelled extensively due to his work. Hema is flooded with memories of the times when Kaushik had moved into their house to stay for a while, till they found their own accommodation.

> "She remembered the ridiculous attraction she had felt that night, when she was thirteen years old, and she had secretly nurtured during the weeks they lived together." (311 GA)

There seemed to be something mysterious between both of them, that at times people around would consider them as lovers. Kaushik drives Hema to his place, where they spend time talking through the day. The slight touches by Kaushik and the attention that he paid to her in the course of the conversation seem to lead to a new bond. There is surge of emotions which were sudden or hidden. The new bond of intimacy and love breaks out between both of them. Hema seems to love every moment, not feeling guilty of her own self and her betrayal towards Navin. She says-

> "Only his kisses, rough, aggressive kisses that were nothing like Navin's schoolboy behaviour at her door... Navin had never looked at her body unclothed, never explored her with his hands, never told her she was beautiful." (313 GA)

> "...... she saw that the area around her lips, at the sides of her mouth, was covered with small red bumps. And she was pleased by that unbecoming proof, pleased that already he had marked her." (314 GA)

Hema and Kaushik had developed a new found love, attraction and intimacy. Nothing seemed to hold them back. They were like newly married couples enjoying the freedom of their relationships. The days passed with both of them spending a lot of time together, exploring places, making love and enjoying the warmth of each other. Hema finds no time to think about her future relationship with Navin. She enjoys every bit of her company with Kaushik.

Even the evening when Navin called to say hi to Hema; the moment passed away into a surge of love making. Although Hema knew that all this would end in a matter of weeks, yet she goes on building up a relation with Kaushik. Hema kept lying to Navin, in order to avoid him from contacting her. She spent more and more time travelling with Kaushik to Voterra.

As they spent time together, one day Kaushik puts forward his proposal,

"Come with me," "To Hong Kong." ".... Don't marry him Hema." (321 GA)

Hema was elated, but at the same time she was also struck by his "selfishness." She seemed to be upset by his dominance here. Shrouded with a sense of helplessness and being in a state of dilemma, Hema rejects his offer. She offers him the idea of being in touch even after marriage, which Kaushik rejects. Hema feels dejected and upset. With that Kaushik and Hema's love affair comes to an end. They depart with heavy hearts.

Hema boards a flight to India and Kaushik moves on with his travel and work.

There seems to be a longing and desire in both of them, but their own limitations do not permit them to bind together.

"He didn't want to leave it up to chance to find her again, didn't want to share her with another man." (326 GA)

As time passes by and with marriage dates to Navin comes closer, Hema is heartbroken the day she hears the news of the disaster that had struck the Indian and Sri Lankan coastline, and Thailand which had been badly affected. She realizes that she had lost Kaushik to this disaster, since his last destination had been Thailand. Sorrow, regret and loss, echoes in her words.

"At the end of that week, Navin arrived to marry me. I was repulsed by the sight of him....."(332 GA)

"I returned to my existence, the existence I had chosen instead of you." (333 GA)

The sensitivity in the Sibling relationship strikes out strong in "Only Goodness." Sudha and Rahul, who belonged to a Bengali family, staying in America. The sibling relationship seems to be like any other universal sibling ties. The fights, the jealousy factor as kids, when the first born feels alienated after the arrival of the second child. The bonding of the siblings is evident as they grow up, the times when they both hide their drinking habits from their parents. Sudha gets her freedom only when she went to Philadelphia for college. Otherwise back home, it was Rahul who was always the apple of the eye. Rahul's going to Cornell was a great event of celebration, which was marked by the presence of nearly two hundred people, in a party that was thrown by the father. The main focus in this sibling relationship is drawn towards the later part of the story, where Sudha is married and Rahul ironically loses his place as the 'apple of the eye', because of his laziness, casualness, and a terrible fall in his higher studies.

> "…..He'd stopped classes, and two weeks ago, after being formally dismissed form the university, he moved back to Wayland." (150 OG)

No amount of parental guidance or sisterly guidance helps Rahul to improve. He becomes more prone to alcoholism and smoking. Sudha tries a lot to help her brother, but her hundred percent is not reflected. Sudha seems to be surrounded with the thoughts of Roger, her new found love and the thoughts of settling down with him in marriage. Rahul approves of the alliance more than the parents, who did not wish for an Englishman for their daughter. But the sensitivity in this sibling relation arises from the episode of the Sudha's marriage reception, where Rahul makes a toast and ruins the big day with his slurred speech in a drunken state.

> "…… but Sudha held her breathe as he spoke, wanting him only to sit down."(156 OG)

Sudha could not forgive her brother for spoiling her special day. The disappearance of Rahul from his home is the next jolt she receives after her wedding; with a follow up news that he had left for Ohio, and did not want to be disturbed any more. Life moves ahead for Sudha with the arrival of her first baby Neel. She grows into fondness with her baby and at times is reminded of her brother too. Days pass by, and to her surprise almost a year and half she receives a letter from Rahul, who apologies for all his weird behaviour and reveals that he had quit all his addictions. The sisterly spirit can't stop her from inviting her brother to her house to see Neel.

Rahul's behaviour throughout seemed to surprise Sudha. He seemed to be more helpful, responsible, a great uncle to Neel and most importantly, he showed no interest in smoking or drinking. Even at dinner,

> "Sudha and Roger had white wine with dinner, but Rahul had asked only club soda mixed with some orange juice." (164 OG)

A day before Rahul was supposed to go back, he proposed Roger and Sudha the idea of going for a movie. He insisted that he would baby sit Neel and do all the needful. Though Sudha was a bit hesitant, yet her changed brother convinced her to go ahead with the plan. In between the movie, Sudha did call up once to check on Neel and Rahul, and she was relieved to know that all was well. On arriving back home after the movie, Sudha could not find any of them, except for the things that were lying all around the place. She felt a sense of nervousness. As she ran up to look upstairs she could hear the water splashing, and felt sorry for having a doubt on her brother. But all her spirits crashed, when she saw Neel in the bath tub all alone, with water reaching his chest, he was playing without the plastic ring around him. She screamed at the sight and Roger rushed to her side and grabbed the baby from the tub. It was a traumatic moment for the couple, which led to a verbal argument about the carelessness of Rahul. They both found him in Roger's study, totally drunk and lying unconscious.To quote

> "They found Rahul in Roger's study, asleep, a glass tucked beneath the daybed. In their bedroom, the sweater chest was open, the necks of bottles poking gout, nestled in woolly arms." (170 OG)

The bad habit of Rahul which Sudha had hid from Roger, lay bare and Roger was wild at Sudha for having lied to him. All night Sudha did not sleep, crying away cursing herself for having trusted her brother. The next morning the shattering of the sibling ties is evident, when Sudha orders Rahul to leave her house immediately. Although, Rahul pretended as though nothing had happened, Sudha was playing the role of a stern sister, a wounded mother, a heartbroken wife. She demanded the exit of her brother from her life and family for ever.

> "You passed out and you left our baby alone in a tub. You could have killed him, do you understand?"(172 OG)

Her words were enough for Rahul to realize the grave mistake he had made, the trust he had broken again.No amount of guilt and reassurance from Rahul, calms Sudha's fury, hurt and rage. The sibling relationship comes crashing down; there is no room for another chance. Sudha's failed trust in her brother brings an end to this relationship for ever.

Pure Love relationships are another integral part of Lahiri's work. She brings about the love relationships which at times succeed as well as fail due to various reasons. One such relationship is evident in the chapter 'Nobody's Business'. The story of three house mates, Sang – who worked at a bookstore, Paul – a Literature student and Heather - a Law student who shared the same apartment. Sang, had numerous calls of suitors, many of whom she kept rejecting for various reasons. As the story progresses she seems to have fallen in love with Farouk, whom Paul happened to see at the sidewalk near the apartment. He seemed to be more sophisticated than Paul driving a bottle-green BMW. Paul observed, -

> "The boyfriend wore perfectly fitted faded jeans, a white shirt, a navy blue blazer and brown leather shoes. His sharp features commanded admiration without being imposing". (185 N'SB)

Something within, makes Paul, uncomfortable and secretly jealous of their relationships. Paul often enjoyed the attention and care he would receive from Sang with regards to his proof readings, or she fixing his doctor's appointments. But there were times when he felt uncomfortable with the presence of the two lovers in the shared apartment. Their presence prompted him to stay away from the apartment. He felt a sense of protectiveness for Sang and became more and more aware of the lovers bonding. He could not help, but, constantly track Sang and Farouk. Once, an argument breaks out between Farouk and Sang. This was overheard by Paul; it appears as though he wanted to take Sang's side who must have been hurt by the proceedings. The first glimpse of longing in Paul is evident at this point of time.

> "A few hours later, Paul nearly bumped into Sang as she was emerging from her bathroom, wrapped in a large pink towel. Her wet hair was uncombed and tangled, a knot bulging like a small nest on one side of her head. For weeks, he had longed to catch a glimpse of her this way and still he felt wholly unprepared for the vision of her bare legs and arms, her damp face and shoulders." (190 N'SB)

Sang had to leave for London, since her sister had a baby. Paul felt that he was able to study better in the absence of Sang. He missed her presence, but at the same time, he felt that her absence helped him to focus better. The element of passionate love is also well displayed in Paul's behaviour, during this period of Sang's absence. One such day he enters Sang's room in her absence, to leave a parcel which had arrived for her, he couldn't help but, linger on in her room.

> "He took off his shoes and socks. On a wine crate next to the futon was a glass of water that had gathered bubbles, a small pot of Vaseline. He undid his belt buckle, but suddenly the desire left him, absent from his body just as she was absent from the room. He buckled his belt again, and then slowly he lifted the bedspread. The sheets were flannel, blue and white, a pattern of fleur-de-lis. He had drifted off to sleep when he heard the phone ring." (193 N'SB)

Paul had yearned for Sang's company, since most of the time Sang was at work or spending time with Farouk or the roommates having their food together. There were very few occasions when Paul got to be in Sang's company.

> "This would be their first dinner together, alone, without Heather. He used to yearn for such an occasion. He used to feel clumsy and tongue-tied when Sang was in the room." (203 N'SB)

Paul's protectiveness and care for Sang becomes more aggressive when he receives a number of phone calls form Deirdre enquiring about Sang's whereabouts in her absence. Her question about Sang and Farouq being cousins surprises him. In a state of intoxication, Deirdre said that she loved Freddy (Farouq). Paul was perplexed and worried, he wanted to hide this information and at the same time save Sang from her fraud partner Farouq. Paul learned a number of secrets from Deirdre over the period of time and that Farouq had been cheating on both Sang and Deirdre. Paul felt that it was his moral responsibility to save Sang from this false relationship. He makes all attempts to make Sang understand that Farouq was cheating on her.

In this process Sang ends up shouting at Paul for interfering in her life. Paul wanted to prove his words true and for this very reason Paul makes the arrangement of getting Deirdre to call him, at a time when Sang would be home from work. He arranges an extension of the phone so that Sang could hear the truth from Deirdre herself. When phone rings and Paul begins the conversation on Farouk, Deirdre opens up all secrets to Paul. Paul proves his loyalty towards Sang, she hears everything through the extension of the phone and is heart broken when she hears the truth. Deirdre says, -

> "Tell her about me and Farouk. She deserves to know. It sounds like you're a good friend of hers." (211 N'SB)

Paul could not bear to see Sang heartbroken; he does not enjoy his victory over Farouq. He laments with Sang, apprehensive, like a true lover, and protector.

> "Deirdre hung up, and for a long time Paul and Sang sat there, listening to the silence.
>
> "He had cleared himself with Sang, and yet he felt no relief, no vindication. ……….After a while he followed her, stood outside. "Sang? Do you need anything?" (211 N'SB)

It appears that Paul was lover who had failed to express his feelings to Sang. Yet, he had stood by her in her difficult times. He had managed to save her from a fraud without seeking any thing in return. His feelings for Sang were never opened up. Sadly, she had left the apartment after the episode of Farouq expose'. It must have been the feeling of pure love which made Paul so involved in her.

II. CONCLUSION:

Lahiri weaves a brilliant web of relationships, which are a part of everyone's life even in the present times. Though the plot of the stories bring about different ideas and themes, but the integral part of these remain the developing and breaking of relationships.

References:

1. Rushdie ,Salman. *"The satanic-verses* .www.enotes.com. 27 Oct 2016
2. Gosh ,A. 2 ed. *"A sea of Poppies"*. New Delhi, Penguin Books, 2008.
3. Martien A. Halvorson-Taylor. " *People related articles /diaspora literature"*. www.bibleodyssey.org. 14 Nov, 2016
4. *"Jhumpa_Lahiri cite note-usa-1"* www.wikipedia.org/wiki, 20 Jan 2016
5. Martien A, Halvorson-Taylor. "Diaspora Literature". 27 Oct 2016.
6. Lahiri Jhumpa. *Unaccustomed Earth.* Random House Publishing company, 2008
7. Minzesheimer, Bob. *"For Pulitzer winner Lahiri, a novel approach"*. USA Today, August 2003
8. Anastas, Benjamin. *"Books: Inspiring Adaptation"*. Men's Vogue, March 2007
9. Ashcroft, Bill, Gareth Griffiths, Tiffin. *"Key Concepts in Post-Colonial Studies"*. London and New York: Routledge, 1998.

YOUR KNOWLEDGE HAS VALUE

- We will publish your bachelor's and master's thesis, essays and papers

- Your own eBook and book - sold worldwide in all relevant shops

- Earn money with each sale

Upload your text at www.GRIN.com and publish for free